Persuasion Workbook

To accompany the text for your Persuasion course

Helen Acosta
John Giertz

Cover image © Shutterstock, Inc. Used under license.

www.kendallhunt.com
Send all inquiries to:
4050 Westmark Drive
Dubuque, IA 52004-1840

Copyright © 2014 by Helen Acosta and John Giertz

ISBN 978-1-5249-8337-6

Kendall Hunt Publishing Company has the exclusive rights to reproduce this work,
to prepare derivative works from this work, to publicly distribute this work,
to publicly perform this work and to publicly display this work.

All rights reserved. No part of this publication may be reproduced,
stored in a retrieval system, or transmitted, in any form or by any
means, electronic, mechanical, photocopying, recording, or otherwise,
without the prior written permission of the copyright owner.

Printed in the United States of America

Contents

Introduction 4

Theories about the Process of Persuasion 5

   Definitions and Foundations of Persuasion 5

   Values, beliefs and attitudes 7

      Values Ranking Worksheet 7

   Models of Communication 9

   Elaboration Likelihood Model (first look) 10

   Aristotle's Rhetoric (in-depth) 11

      Ethos 11

      Pathos 12

      Logos 13

      Relational Model of Aristotle's Ethos, Pathos, Logo 14

   Behavior and Persuasion 15

      Nonverbal Persuaders 15

      Behavioral theories 16

      Application Activity: The Meth Project 20

   Theories about the role of symbolic expression in persuasion 21

      Semiotics (Saussure and Eco) 22

      Application Activity: Clean jokes and language choice 23

   Logical Reasoning in Persuasion 24

      Application Activity: Find the fallacies in a letter to the editor 27

   Marketing Models of Persuasion 28

      Application Activity: Rank Model of Persuasion 28

      Application Activity: Analyzing an historic ad campaign 32

Methods and Tools to Prepare Speeches 35

   Audience Analysis: Before you write your speech get to know your audience 35

      Demographics. Audience Analysis: Class Survey 35

      Psychographics 36

      Audience analysis websites 37

      Audience Analysis Process 38

      Sample Questionnaire with Results 40

   Outlining 44

    Standard Speech Structure 44

    Standard Speech Outline Template (Label these elements in your TYPED outline) 46

    Outlining Activity 48

    Patterns of Organization: Ways to organize a speech body 49

    Persuasion Outlines: Policy Propositions 50

    How to Prepare a Well-Developed Speech Introduction 51

    How to Prepare a Well-Developed Speech Conclusion 52

Supporting materials 53

    Where to use SUPPORTING MATERIALS in your speech 53

    Public Speaking Citations/Resources Standards Sheet 54

    Example of Raw Research 55

    Example of Paraphrased Research in Oral Citation Format 56

    Evaluation of Web Information 57

    Stories or Verbal Illustrations 58

    Statistics 59

Visual Aids 60

    Why should a speaker use visual aids? 60

    Public Speaking Presentation Aids Standards Sheet 61

    Presentation aids using Presentation Software 64

Language 65

    Effective Language Tools for Oral Presentations 65

    Transitional Words 66

    When to use Transition Words 67

Personal Reporting of Communication Apprehension (PRCA) 68

Dedication

This workbook is dedication to all of the students who have taken Persuasion at Bakersfield College since the course began a decade ago.

Introduction

This workbook has been organized in two sections:

- Theories about the Process of Persuasion
- Methods and Tools to Prepare for Speeches

There are many theories about the process of persuasion. In this workbook you will be introduced to just a few of the most enduring. You will find the answers to the many questions about these theories in your text and on-line.

In your Persuasion class you will be required to give a minimum of 3 substantive, prepared speeches. The speaking times will vary for each speech. However, over the course of the semester you should expect to speak for a minimum of 22 minutes. At least 2 of your speeches will require you do to research, both in the Library and on-line.

While the class does require you to engage with theories and give speeches you will find that this class is one where you will come to know your classmates well and have fun along the way!

Enjoy!

Theories about the Process of Persuasion

Definitions and Foundations of Persuasion

Write out the definition of "persuasion" that is most appealing to you:

_____

_____

_____

_____

List the 3 major elements of this definition that best clarify the functions of persuasion:

1)_____

_____

2)_____

_____

3)_____

_____

Aristotle's *Rhetoric* is often credited as the most important set of texts on persuasion ever written. The *Rhetoric* is composed of 3 books. Find the below foundational concepts of Aristotle's *Rhetoric* in your text.

Aristotle defines *rhetoric* as:_____

_____

_____

Aristotle defines *logos* as: _____

_____

_____

Persuasion Workbook

Aristotle defines *ethos* as: _____

_____

_____

Aristotle defines *pathos* as: _____

_____

_____

What are some of the differences between the author's main definitions of persuasion and Aristotle's?

_____

_____

_____

Do the author(s) include new or additional concepts, opposing views, leave out some of Aristotle's views, etc?

_____

_____

_____

_____

Values, beliefs and attitudes

What is a value?_____
_____
_____

How are values formed?_____
_____
_____

What is a belief?_____
_____
_____

How are beliefs formed?_____
_____
_____

What is an attitude?_____
_____
_____

How are attitudes formed?_____
_____
_____

Values Ranking Worksheet
Circle the values listed below that you would most like others to see in you.

Accountability	Calmness	Continuous Improvement
Accuracy	Carefulness	Contribution
Achievement	Challenge	Control
Adventurousness	Cheerfulness	Cooperation
Altruism	Clear-mindedness	Correctness
Ambition	Commitment	Courtesy
Assertiveness	Community	Creativity
Balance	Compassion	Curiosity
Being the best	Competitiveness	Decisiveness
Belonging	Consistency	Dependability
Boldness	Contentment	Determination

Persuasion Workbook

Devoutness	Honesty	Results-oriented
Diligence	Honor	Rigor
Discipline	Humility	Security
Discretion	Inclusive	Self-actualization
Diversity	Independence	Self-control
Dynamism	Ingenuity	Selflessness
Economy	Inner Harmony	Self-reliance
Effectiveness	Inquisitiveness	Sensitivity
Efficiency	Insightfulness	Serenity
Elegance	Intelligence	Service
Empathy	Intellectual Status	Shrewdness
Enjoyment	Intuition	Simplicity
Enthusiasm	Joy	Soundness
Equality	Justice	Speed
Excellence	Leadership	Spontaneity
Excitement	Legacy	Stability
Expertise	Love	Strategic
Exploration	Loyalty	Strength
Expressiveness	Making a difference	Structure
Fairness	Mastery	Success
Faith	Merit	Support
Family-focused	Obedience	Teamwork
Fidelity	Openness	Temperance
Fitness	Order	Thankfulness
Fluency	Originality	Thoroughness
Focus	Patriotism	Thoughtfulness
Freedom	Perfection	Timeliness
Fun	Piety	Tolerance
Generosity	Positivity	Traditionalism
Goodness	Practicality	Trustworthiness
Grace	Preparedness	Truth-seeking
Growth	Professionalism	Understanding
Happiness	Prudence	Uniqueness
Hard Work	Quality-orientation	Unity
Health	Reliability	Usefulness
Helping Society	Resourcefulness	Vision
Holiness	Restraint	Vitality

List your top three values from above and explain why each value is important to you.

1. _____

    _____

2. _____

    _____

3. _____

    _____

Models of Communication

Name:_____ Class day/s_____ Class hour_____

Draw the SMCR model of communication in the box below.

Shannon and Weaver's SMCR Model of Communication

Extra Credit: Draw the Transaction Model of Communication in the box below.

Transactional Model of Communication

Name:_____ Class day/s_____ Class hour_____

Elaboration Likelihood Model (first look)

Create your own diagram to show the relationship between the important elements of the Elaboration Likelihood Model. Draw your diagram below or create your diagram using your favorite program then print and bring to class. Be prepared to discuss your model in class—possibly in a small group or in a class discussion

Aristotle's Rhetoric (in-depth)

Ethos

Aristotle discussed *phronesis*. What is *phronesis*? _____
_____
_____

Aristotle discussed *arete*. What is *arete*? _____
_____
_____

Aristotle discussed *eunoia*. What is *eunoia*? _____
_____
_____

While speakers can work to build their ethos, ultimately ethos is conferred by whom?
_____

Ways to Build your ETHOS

Building ethos throughout your life:
Be a good person (trustworthiness), only speak on topics about which you have gained expertise (reputation), build the brand that is you (reputation), work to relate to people based on their needs and interests (similarity).

In speaking situations—before you speak:
Get to know individuals in the audience: show up early, build shared experience (trustworthiness), dress for the occasion and audience (similarity), dress to emphasize your field of expertise (authority).

In speaking situations—during your speech:
Tell stories and anecdotes that are consistent with your message (trustworthiness), use language that is familiar to your audience (similarity), use visuals and examples that reflect audience experience (similarity), choose examples and statistics from sources your audience trusts (trustworthiness, authority, similarity), reference people your audience knows and/or trusts (similarity).

After you speak
Make yourself available to the audience for follow-up after the presentation (similarity), follow-through on promises made during the presentation (trustworthiness).

Persuasion Workbook

Pathos

What are hot and cold words? _____
_____

How might hot and cold words be used to build pathos? _____
_____

What dangers should speakers be aware of when they choose to use hot and cold words? _____
_____
_____

How might analogies, metaphors and other figures of speech be used to build pathos? _____
_____
_____

How might stories be used to build pathos? _____
_____
_____

What is the *known identifiable victim effect*? _____
_____
_____

How might the *known identifiable victim effect* build pathos? _____
_____
_____

How might visual presentation aids be used to build pathos? _____
_____

What delivery techniques might you use to build pathos? _____
_____
_____

Logos

What is *deductive reasoning*? _____
_____
_____

What is *inductive reasoning*? _____
_____
_____

What is a syllogism? _____
_____
_____

Write a syllogism on the 3 lines below:

_____
_____
_____

What is an enthymeme? _____
_____
_____

Write an enthymeme on the 2 lines below:

_____
_____

How might charts and diagrams be used to build logos? _____
_____
_____

Relational Model of Aristotle's Ethos, Pathos, Logo
Draw a model that shows the elements of Aristotle's Ethos, Pathos and Logos that focuses on 1) the relationship between the elements and 2) the relative importance of each element.

Behavior and Persuasion

Nonverbal Persuaders

Visit Youtube and type in "Cartoons on the Rights of the Child Articles 1-20" watch the videos. Then type in "Cartoons of the Rights of the Child Articles 21-54", watch the videos. Choose the video that you felt was the most persuasive.

Child Rights video title:_____

Nation of origin:_____

Circle the 2 nonverbal behaviors that were the most persuasive elements of your chosen cartoon:

Facial Expression	Gestures	Paralinguistics	Body Language and Posture
Proxemics	Eye Gaze	Haptics	Appearance

Circled behavior #1_____

Define the term listed in #1_____

_____

_____

Why was this behavior persuasive in the cartoon?

_____

_____

_____

_____

Circled behavior #2_____

Define the term listed in #2_____

_____

_____

Why was this behavior persuasive in the cartoon?

_____

_____

_____

Persuasion Workbook

Behavioral theories

Explain the *stimulus response* aka *operant conditioning* theory: _____
_____

Who was Pavlov? _____
_____

What was his famous experience that proved his theory of operant conditioning? _____
_____
_____
_____

Explain *inoculation theory*: _____
_____

What was the situation that lead to the development of inoculation theory? _____
_____
_____
_____

When might inoculation theory be useful to you or people you know? _____
_____
_____

Explain *attribution theory*: _____
_____
_____

What are the possible drawbacks of attribution theory? _____
_____
_____

Explain the *boomerang effect* (not to be confused with the boomerang method of persuasion): _____

_____

_____

_____

_____

Give an example of an ad campaign that suffered from the boomerang effect: _____

_____

_____

Explain *social judgment theory*: _____

_____

_____

_____

_____

Type "Social Judgment Theory Sherif" into a search engine query box. Choose images. Look through the many different models provided to visualize the Social Judgment Theory. Choose the model that provides the greatest clarity for you. Draw the model below.

Explain *normative social influence*: _____

_____

_____

_____

_____

Give an example from your own life in which normative social influence changed your behavior or someone else's behavior: _____

_____

_____

_____

Explain *the heuristic-systemic model of persuasion*: _____

_____

_____

_____

Type "Heuristic-systemic persuasion model" into a search engine query box. Choose images. Look through the many different models provided to visualize the Social Judgment Theory. Choose the model that provides the greatest clarity for you. Draw the model below.

Persuasion Workbook

Explain *Ajzen's Theory of Planned Behavior:* _____
_____
_____
_____
_____

How does Ajzen's Theory of Planned Behavior help us to better predict people's future behaviors?
_____
_____
_____
_____
_____

Explain *Festinger's Theory of Cognitive Dissonance:* _____
_____
_____
_____
_____
_____

Give an example from your own life in which cognitive dissonance played a role:_____
_____
_____
_____
_____
_____

Explain *Affect Perseverance*: _____
_____
_____
_____
_____

How does Affect Perseverance differ from Cognitive Dissonance? :_____

Persuasion Workbook

_____
_____
_____
_____
_____

Application Activity: The Meth Project

Type the following into a search engine: methproject.org ads
Watch the ads. Choose the ad that you think is the most persuasive.

Name of ad:_____

Type the following into a search engine: meth project fact sheet pdf
List the 3 most persuasive supports provided on the fact sheet.

1)_____
_____

2)_____
_____

3)_____
_____

Think about the ad your chose above as well as the supports you listed from the fact sheet. Circle the theory that best explains the success of the Meth Project:

Inoculation Theory	Attribution Theory	Social Judgment Theory
Normative Social Influence	Heuristic-Systemic Model	Theory of Planned Behavior
Cognitive Dissonance	Affect Perseverance	

Why does the theory you circled explain the success of the Meth Project more effectively than any of the other listed theories?

_____
_____
_____
_____
_____

Theories about the role of symbolic expression in persuasion

How did Susanne Langer view symbolic expression? _____
_____
_____
_____

What did she say the role of shared symbol systems is in communities? _____
_____
_____

Kenneth Burke said that: "Man is the symbol-_____ (symbol-_____,

symbol-_____) animal,

inventor of the _____ (or moralized by the _____),

_____ from his natural condition by _____ of his own making,

goaded by the spirit of _____ (or moved by the sense of _____),

and rotten _____"

Kenneth Burke believed that every action is symbolic and that all actions are persuasive. He developed the Dramatistic Pentad in order to analyze the persuasive motives present in any situation. List and explain the 5 elements of the pentad.

1) _____
_____

2) _____
_____

3) _____
_____

4) _____
_____

5) _____
_____

Semiotics (Saussure and Eco)

In Saussure and Eco's studies of Semiotics what is "sign"?
_____
_____
_____

What is a Signifier?
_____
_____

Circle the aspect of language it is most related to: Verbal   Nonverbal

What is a Signified?
_____
_____

Circle the aspect of language it is most related to: Verbal   Nonverbal

Explain denotative meaning :_____
_____
_____

Denotative meaning (Circle the correct answer):   Signifier   Signified

Explain connotative meaning :_____
_____
_____

Denotative meaning (Circle the correct answer):   Signifier   Signified

Possible Extra Credit: Provide a semiotic analysis of a merchandizing or political ad. Be sure to identify the sign, signifier(s) and signified(s). Ask instructor for more details.

Application Activity: Clean jokes and language choice

Visit FunnyJokes.com and choose a joke that you find funny and would feel comfortable telling in class.

Write out the joke_____

_____

_____

_____

_____

_____

Circle the use of language (found at changingminds.org) that best explains why the joke works:

Amplification	Reduction	Dead metaphor
Distortion	Reference	Dormant metaphor
Emotion	Repetition	Dying metaphor
Excess	Reversal	Extended metaphor
Falsehood	Sound	Implicit metaphor
Reversal	Substitution	Mixed metaphor
Hidden meaning	Absolute metaphor	Pataphor
Meaning	Active metaphor	Root metaphor
Omission	Complex metaphor	Simple metaphor
Questioning	Compound metaphor	Submerged metaphor
Rearrangement	Concrete metaphor	Synechdochic metaphor

Explain the concept that you circled above_____

_____

_____

_____

Why does this concept make the joke work? _____

_____

_____

_____

Persuasion Workbook

Logical Reasoning in Persuasion

Beyond the early discussion of logos found on pages 9-11 in this workbook, the primary stumbling blocks persuaders encounter are the result of fallacious reasoning. Below, explain each of the forms of fallacious reasoning (help can be found at yourlogicalfallacyis.com).

Strawman _____
_____
_____

False Cause _____
_____
_____

Appeal to Emotion _____
_____
_____

The Fallacy Fallacy _____
_____
_____

Slippery Slope _____
_____
_____

Ad Hominem _____
_____
_____

Tu Quoque _____
_____
_____

Personal
Incredulity _____

Persuasion Workbook

_____
_____

Special Pleading_____
_____
_____

Loaded Question_____
_____
_____

Burden of Proof_____
_____
_____

Ambiguity_____
_____
_____

The Gambler's Fallacy_____
_____
_____

Bandwagon_____
_____
_____

Appeal to Authority_____
_____
_____

Composition/Division_____
_____
_____

Persuasion Workbook

No True Scotsman _____
_____
_____

Genetic _____
_____
_____

Black or White _____
_____
_____

Begging the Question _____
_____
_____

Appeal to Nature _____
_____
_____

Anecdotal _____
_____
_____

The Texas Sharpshooter _____
_____
_____

Middle Ground _____
_____
_____

Application Activity: Find the fallacies in a letter to the editor

Visit the website for your local newspaper and find the most recent letters to the editor. Choose one letter in which the writer fell prey, at least twice, to 2 different types of fallacious reasoning.

Title of the letter_____

Topic of the letter_____

First type of fallacious reasoning the letter writer fell prey to:

_____

Transcribe the part of the letter in which the writer fell prey to the above type of fallacious reasoning:

_____

_____

_____

_____

Explain why this part of the letter is an excellent example of the fallacy listed above.

_____

_____

_____

_____

Second type of fallacious reasoning the letter writer fell prey to:

_____

Transcribe the part of the letter in which the writer fell prey to the above type of fallacious reasoning:

_____

_____

_____

Explain why this part of the letter is an excellent example of the fallacy listed above.

_____

_____

_____

_____

Marketing Models of Persuasion

Application Activity: Rank Model of Persuasion
Hugh Rank developed a model of persuasion to analyze marketing media that is based on the contrasts between intensifying the selling points of a product and downplaying the aspects of a product that might make the consumer turn against a product.

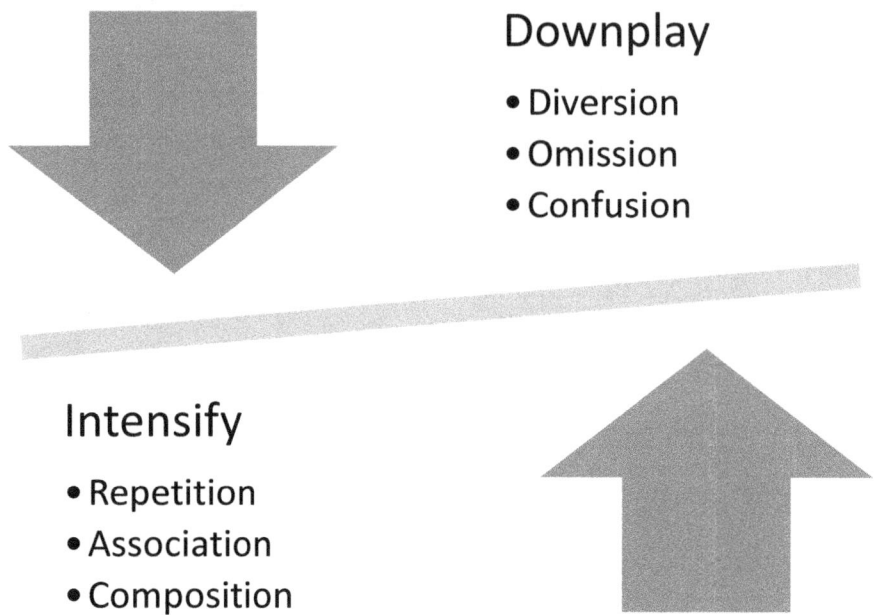

Activity: Visit Youtube. Type in: "2014 Superbowl Ads". Choose one ad to analyze using the Rank Model of Persuasion.

The name of your chosen ad:_____

How do the advertisers **divert** our attention from negative aspects of this product?

_____
_____
_____
_____

What, about the product, do the advertisers **omit** in order to downplay negative aspects of this product?

_____
_____
_____
_____

Persuasion Workbook

How do the advertisers **confuse** us in order to downplay negative aspects of the product?

_____
_____
_____
_____

What do the advertisers **repeat** in the ad in order to intensify our interest in the product?

_____
_____
_____
_____

What do the advertisers want us to **associate** the product with in order to intensify our interest in the product?

_____
_____
_____
_____

How do the advertisers **compose** the ad visually to draw us in and intensify our interest in the product? This should be a description of what you SAW in the ad.

_____
_____
_____
_____
_____
_____
_____

Persuasion Workbook

List and explain the parts of the Yale 5 Stage Developmental Model

1) _____
_____
_____

2) _____
_____
_____

3) _____
_____
_____

4) _____
_____
_____

5) _____
_____

List and explain the 6 steps of the Hierarchy of Effects Model

1) _____
_____
_____

2) _____
_____
_____

3) _____
_____

4) _____

_____

_____

5) _____

_____

6) _____

_____

Define ToMA _____

_____

_____

Why is ToMA important? _____

_____

_____

Persuasion Workbook

Application Activity: Analyzing an historic ad campaign

Look through the list of 40 ad campaigns at the end of this activity and choose 1 to analyze.

Name of the ad campaign_____

Find videos of the campaign on YouTube and do some research about the campaign to answer the following questions:

What was the duration of the campaign?_____

What was the central message of the campaign? _____

_____

_____

Who was the target audience for the campaign? _____

_____

_____

How did the campaign connect with the target audience?_____

_____

_____

Circle the model that best explains the success of the campaign:

      Yale 5 Stage Developmental Model   Hierarchy of Effects Model

List and explain the 3 parts of the model you circled above that are most important to the success of the campaign:

Part 1:_____

_____

_____

_____

Part 2:_____

_____

_____

_____

Draw the model you chose (either Yale 5 Stage Developmental Model or Hierarchy of Effects Model). Apply the elements of your chosen ad campaign to the elements of the model.

40 Ad Campaigns that made or saved the brand

1. 7-up, "The Un-Cola"
2. Absolute Vodka, "Absolute Bottle"
3. Alka Seltzer, "Plop, plop, fizz, fizz: Oh what a relief it is!"
4. Apple "Get a Mac"
5. Apple, "Think Different"
6. Barack Obama, "Yes We Can"
7. BMW, "The ultimate driving machine"
8. Budweiser, "This Bud's for You"
9. Burger King, "Have it your way"
10. Burma Shave, roadway signs in verse
11. Charmin, "Don't squeeze the Charmin"
12. Clairol, "Does She or Doesn't She"
13. Coke, "I'd like to teach the world to sing"
14. DeBeers, "A Diamond is Forever"
15. Dos Equis, "The most interesting man in the World"
16. Dove, "Real Beauty"
17. Federal Express, "Absolutely, Positively Overnight"
18. Greyhound, "Leave the driving to us"
19. Jack Links, "Messin' with Sasquatch"
20. Jello, Bill Cosby with kids
21. Las Vegas, "What happens in Vegas, stays in Vegas"
22. Levis Jeans, "501 Blues"
23. M & M's, "Melt in your mouth, not in your hands"
24. Marlboro, "The Marlboro Man"
25. Maytag, "A Maytag repairman is the loneliest guy in town"
26. Mc Donald's, "You deserve a break today"
27. Miller Lite, "Tastes Great, Less Filling"
28. Morton Salt, "When it Rains, It pours"
29. Motel 6, "We'll leave the light on for you"
30. National Dairy Council, "Got Milk?"
31. Nike, "Just Do It"
32. Old Spice, "The Man Your Man Could Smell Like"
33. Priceline, "The Priceline Negotiator featuring William Shatner"
34. Proactive, Celebrity Endorsements
35. Progressive Insurance, "Flo the Progressive Girl"
36. Reese's Pieces, "ET"
37. Ronald Reagan, "Morning in America"
38. US Army, "Be all that you can be"
39. Volkswagen, "think small"
40. Wendy's, "Where's the Beef"

Ad campaigns that hurt the brand

The Taco Bell Chihuahua

The Energizer Bunny

California Raisins, "Heard it through the grapevine"

Alka Seltzer, "Meatballs"

Sony PSP, "Black vs. White"

Mc Donald's, "I'd hit it!"

Groupon, "Tibet"

Methods and Tools to Prepare Speeches

Audience Analysis: Before you write your speech get to know your audience

Demographics. Audience Analysis: Class Survey
Examples of demographic information:

1. What is your age:
   - ☐ under 18 years
   - ☐ between 18-25 years
   - ☐ between 26-35 years
   - ☐ over 36 years

2. Are you
   - ☐ male
   - ☐ female

3. With which race or ethnicity do you most identify?
   - ☐ White/Caucasian
   - ☐ Black/African
   - ☐ Asian/Pacific Islander
   - ☐ American Native
   - ☐ Hispanic
   - ☐ Other

4. What is your religious affiliation—if any?
   - ☐ Protestant
   - ☐ Catholic
   - ☐ Other Christian
   - ☐ Buddhist
   - ☐ Hindu
   - ☐ Muslim
   - ☐ Atheist
   - ☐ Other_____

5. Marital status:
   - ☐ married
   - ☐ single
   - ☐ divorced
   - ☐ co-habitating

6. Do you have children?
   - ☐ none
   - ☐ 1
   - ☐ 2
   - ☐ 3
   - ☐ 4
   - ☐ 5
   - ☐ 6 or more

7. Do you work while attending school? ☐ no ☐ yes
   if yes:
   - ☐ fewer than 10 hours per week
   - ☐ 10-19 hours per week
   - ☐ 20-29 hours per week
   - ☐ 30-39 hours per week
   - ☐ 40 hours per week
   - ☐ 40+ hours per week

8. Is English your first language? ☐ yes ☐ no
9. Were you born outside of California? ☐ yes ☐ no
10. Were you born outside the continental United States? ☐ yes ☐ no
11. Have you traveled outside of California? ☐ yes ☐ no

12. Have you traveled outside of the United States? ☐ yes ☐ no
13. Have you visited Disneyland? ☐ yes ☐ no

14. What is your educational goal?
    - ☐ To survive BC and stay on Mom's/Dad's health insurance plan
    - ☐ A certificate or vocational program
    - ☐ Transfer to a four year college and earn a Bachelor's degree
    - ☐ Graduate school for a Master's degree
    - ☐ A terminal degree (PhD. JD EdD, etc..)

15. Is your political affiliation:
    - ☐ Republican
    - ☐ Democrat
    - ☐ Libertarian
    - ☐ Green
    - ☐ "Decline to State" (in California "Independent" is the American Independent Party)
    - ☐ Other
    - ☐ None

Psychographics (will your audience's views on any of the following impact your success?)

EDUCATION
College Loans debt out-of-control?
Is D.A.R.E. effective?
Are Standardized Tests helpful?
Tablets vs. Textbooks
Teacher Tenure

ELECTIONS & PRESIDENTS
Felon Voting
Electronic Voting Machines

HEALTH & MEDICINE
Abortion
Euthanasia
Medical Marijuana
Obamacare / Health Care
Prescription Drug Ads to Consumers
Right to Health Care
Vaccines for Kids

MEDIA & ENTERTAINMENT
Social Networking
Video Games and Violence

MONEY & BUSINESS
Big Three Auto Bailout
Corporate Tax Rate & Jobs
Gold Standard
Insider Trading by Congress

POLITICS
Concealed Handguns
Death Penalty
Drinking Age
Immigration Reform
Social Security Privatization

RELIGION
Churches and Taxes
Under God in the Pledge
Should Atheists run for public office?

SCIENCE & TECHNOLOGY
Alternative Energy vs. Fossil Fuels
Animal Testing
Climate Change

SEX & GENDER
Born Gay? Origins of Sexual Orientation
Same Sex Marriage
Legalizing Prostitution

SPORTS
Should college athletes players be paid?
Drug Use in Sports

WORLD / INTERNATIONAL
Cuba Embargo
Drones
Israeli-Palestinian Conflict

There will be times that you need to know where an audience stands on an issue prior to speaking. Being forewarned is being prepared. Imagine that you have prepared a speech about reasons to require navy blue school uniforms—and then find out that your audience is opposed to any policy requiring school uniforms.

Persuasion Workbook

Analysis

Understanding

Demographics

Interest

Environment

Needs

Customized

Expectations

Audience analysis websites
US Census
www.census.gov

Gallup Polls
www.gallup.com

Pew Research Center
www.people-press.org

National Election Studies

http://www.electionstudies.org/

Advertising Age, American Demographics
www.adage.com/americandemographics/

Bakersfield College Student Demographic Trends

From the BC Office of Institutional Research and Planning, Data, Where we are, 2012-13:
- Ethnicity

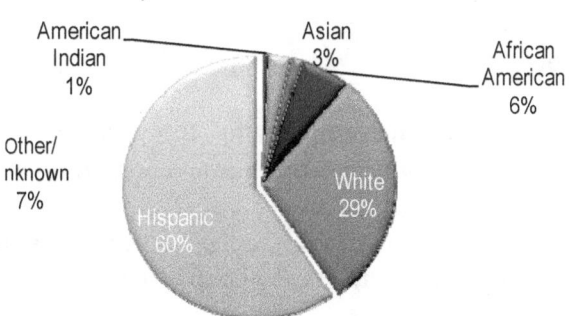

- Gender: 54.5% Female, 45.2% Male, .7% unknown
- Load: 30.5% Full-time, 69.9% part-time

Audience Analysis Process

Your basic purpose is to find out the audience's attitude toward your topic and what they think of your possible solutions.

You will measure three aspects:

1. The audience's understanding of the topic

2. The audience's disposition toward the topic

3. The audience's willingness to go along with your solution

Each of the above categories overlaps yet you want to measure them separately.

Types of questions for measuring the understanding

The first type is called a *fixed-response question* because you don't allow the audience to have any range on the answers. For example, this question allows you to find out, in general, if the audience feels they know about the insanity plea.

"Do you know what the insanity plea is in the U.S. legal system?

YES_____

NO_____

Not Sure_____

This does not measure whether the audience ACTUALLY knows much about the insanity plea, just whether, in general, they have an understanding.

The next type of question, *a scale question*, helps to measure the audience's attitude toward the topic; e.g., do they like it, do they oppose it, are they comfortable with it, or whatever else you ask them.

Do you agree or disagree with the following statement: On a scale of 1 to 5,(1 being strongly agree and 5 being strongly disagree) "To the extent possible, people have an obligation to help those in less fortunate circumstances?"

Strongly Agree   Mildly Agree   Undecided   Mildly Disagree   Strongly Disagree

_____1_____|_____2____|____3____|____4_____|____5_____

Notice that I gave a definition of the numbering system and the numbers also line up with key words. The scale questions should always be set up with opposite but EQUAL measurements on the far ends.

To measure the audience's willingness to go along with your solution you can ask them their attitude toward it in a scale question like given above. You can also ask them an *open-ended question* which doesn't put restrictions on their answers. Try to put the respondents into a scenario dealing with your topic without actually stating your point of view. For example:

If you have worked as a volunteer, do you plan to do so again and why? (It is necessary to include the phrase "and why" otherwise people will answer a simple yes or no with no explanation)

If a loved one were in the hospital and in great physical pain, would you want life support discontinued, if so by whom. If not, why not?

SAMPLE QUESTIONNAIRE:

1. Have you ever been ticketed for speeding?

   1. Yes. 2. No

2. Do you regularly speed?

   1. Yes. 2. No

3. On a scale of 1 to 5 with 1 being not at all serious and 5 being very serious; how serious is speeding to you?

1	2	3	4	5
(Not at all serious)	(Hardly serious)	(Not an issue)	(Serious)	(Very Serious)

4. On a scale of 1 to 5 with 1 being not effective and 5 being effective; how effective are speeding tickets in reducing speeding?

1	2	3	4	5
(Never effective)	(Rarely effective)	(Occasionally Effective)	(Sometimes effective)	(Always effective)

5. Open ended question.

If you were the victim of a non-death speeding accident, what would you want to happen to the guilty party?

Persuasion Workbook

Sample Questionnaire with Results

Before you create your questionnaire you want to think about what you need to find out from your audience. You want to know if they are confused about your previous work, if they are concerned, if they agree or disagree with your position and how they feel about your potential solution. Think of what type of persuasion you are trying to accomplish. There are three different types: people who agree, people who are unsure, and people who disagree. Each type demands a different approach from you, in other words, a different type of outline.

This form below demonstrates the question format I want you to use for your questionnaire.

1. Use five to six questions: 2 fixed-response, 2 scale, no more than 1 open-ended. (Plus gender and age if this information is needed.)

2. Fixed-Response questions are designed to measure a fixed response between two or more responses. These questions establish the listeners' level of knowledge about and degree of involvement with the topic. For Example:

"Do you know what the insanity plea is in the U.S. legal system?

YES_____

NO_____

Not Sure_____

"Do you know of any legal cases in which the insanity plea was used?

YES_____

NO_____

NOT SURE_____

By limiting the possible responses, such questions produce clear, unambiguous answers. They also tend to yield superficial answers. Other types of questions are needed to get beneath the surface.

Scale questions resemble fixed-alternative questions, but they allow more leeway in responding. Scale questions can also measure the attitude of listeners' toward your topic. (Refer back to the Social Judgment theory on page 85).

How often do you believe the insanity plea is used in U.S. courts?

Very seldom   Very often

_____|_____|_____|_____|_____

Do you agree or disagree with the following statement: To the extent possible, people have an obligation to help those in less fortunate circumstances?

Strongly Agree   Mildly Agree   Undecided   Mildly Disagree   Strongly Disagree

_____|_____|_____|_____|_____

The answers to these questions will help you determine the "Anchor" point of your audience. You can also break down your audience into subgroups based on demographics to see if that has an impact.

(Notice there are five actual spaces for responses ranging from very seldom to very often or from Strongly Agree to Strongly Disagree. The scale is set up to provide the extremes on each end and the middle is reserved for "unsure." Set up your scale questions with 5 responses possible and the extremes--written on the questionnaire--at either end.)

Scale questions must be worded so that the opposite ends are worded the same. You can't have 1 being "Never Agree" and 5 being "Usually agree" because these responses do not carry equal and opposite weight. Therefore, they won't equally counterbalance.

The open-ended question allows the audience to respond however they want. The open-ended questions help gauge the audience's disposition toward your topic and possible solution. Try to put the respondents into a scenario dealing with your topic without actually stating your point of view. For example:

If you have worked as a volunteer, do you plan to do so again and why? (It is necessary to include the phrase "and why" otherwise people will answer a simple yes or no with no explanation)

If a loved one were in the hospital and in great physical pain, would you want life support discontinued, if so by whom. If not, why not?

You may also ask gender, age, if these seem relevant to your topic.

SAMPLE QUESTIONNAIRE:

1. Have you ever been ticketed for speeding:

    1. Yes.   2. No

2. Do you regularly speed?

    1. Yes.   2. No

Persuasion Workbook

3. On a scale of 1 to 5 with 1 being not at all serious and 5 being very serious; how serious is speeding to you?

       1   2   3   4   5

(Not at all serious) (Hardly serious) (Not an issue) (Serious) (Very Serious)

4. On a scale of 1 to 5 with 1 being not fair and 5 being fair; how fair are speeding tickets?

       1   2   3   4   5

(Never fair) (Rarely fair) (undecided) (Sometimes Fair) (Almost always fair)

What is wrong with the above scale?

5. Open ended question.

If you were the victim of a non-death speeding accident, what would you want to happen to the guilty party?

QUESTIONNAIRE "RAW" DATA

	Yes	No	Total		
Q1: Ticketed for speeding	5 / 25%	15 /75%	20/ 100%		
Q2: Regularly Speed?	15/75%	5/25%	20/ 100%		
Q3: How Serious?	#1/ 4	#2/ 5	#3 /5	#4/ 3	#5/ 3
Q4: How fair?	#1/ 8	#2/ 6	#3/2	#4/ 4	#5/ 0

QUESTIONNAIRE COMPARISON DATA

Q1: Have you ever been ticketed for speeding?	yes	no
Q1/Q3: On a scale of 1-5, How serious is breaking the speed limit? 1=not at all serious, 5=very serious	Average Score (3.5)	Average Score (2.0)
Q1: Have you ever been ticketed for speeding?	yes	no
Q1/Q4: On a scale of 1-5, how fair are speeding tickets? 1=not at all fair, 5=very fair	2.2	4.9

Q2: Do you regularly speed on Freeways?	Yes	No
Q2/Q3: On a scale of 1-5, How serious is breaking the speed limit?	1.2	3.0

What to do with this information:

You will analyze the data to come to some broad conclusions. How to find the averages:

The basic formula is multiply each column by the amount of responses and divide by the total number of respondents. Below is a table for the answers to a possible scale questions. The top row has the possible choices, the second row has the total number of people who selected that choice, and the final row is for determining the average choice. The colored columns indicate the information you will need to multiply

Choice #	1	2	3	4	5	
Amount	5	7	0	8	8	
Total	5	14	0	32	40	91

First, you will multiple each column. Choice 1 has 5 responses for a total of 5 points. 1x5 =5. Choice 2 has 7 responses for a multiplied total of 142x7=14. Next, 3x0=0, 4x8=32, and 5x8=40. Add the total. This is 5+14+0+32+40 = 91.

Second, divide the total number--91 by the total number of respondents--29. 91/29= 3.13. So, the average is 3.13

Third, Notice the average choice is 3.13 but no one picked three as their choice. The choices were located closer to the anchor positions, So the audience is very opinionated about this questions

Warning, you cannot just add all the choices and divide by the total number of questionnaires.

Outlining

Standard Speech Structure

Regardless of the general purpose of your speech, there are several elements which remain consistent. In order for listeners to follow your train of thinking, always try to adhere to the "golden rule" of public speaking. (i.e., 1. Tell them what you're going to tell them. 2. Tell them. 3. Tell them what you told them.)

Introduction

The introduction should serve to set up the rest of the speech for listeners. (In the "golden rule" of public speaking this is the "Tell them what you're going to tell them" part.)

I. **Attention Catcher** (This statement serves two functions: it catches listeners' attention and tunes them into your topic. You may use a rhetorical question, a direct question, a humorous anecdote, a famous quotation, a hypothetical example, an actual example, a startling statistic, and so on.)

II. **Establish Relationships** (In this section you help your audience connect with you and the topic.)
    A. **Listener Relevance** (Once you have your listeners' attention, you need to reveal why they should listen to this particular speech. How does this material affect them? Why should they care?)

    B. **Speaker Credibility** (In this step, you need to let listeners know why they should listen to you in particular. How/Why do you know more about this topic than they do? You may have personal experience with the topic; you may have researched extensively; you may have written articles about the topic. The point is, let your listeners know at the outset that you know a good deal about the topic.)

III. **Preview the Message**
    A. **Thesis Statement** (This one-sentence summary of your speech is formed by, first, combining the general purpose to inform, to persuade, to entertain, to introduce, and the specific purpose about what? Be sure to state your thesis quite clearly. If listeners miss this part, they will have difficulty following the rest of the speech.)

    B. **Preview** (In this statement, alert your listeners to the main points of your speech. As with the thesis statement, be very clear so listeners can easily follow the organizational pattern of the speech.)

Body

(In the "golden rule," this is the "Tell them." part.)

I. **First main point** (this is the first main idea that you mentioned in the preview)

   A. Subpoint (These supporting points help listeners understand your perspective. They learn why you stated your main point the way you did. Consider breadth, depth, and listener relevance as you support each main point.)
   B. Subpoint

Transition (Verbally tie the two main points together, in this case the first and second main points, so that listeners know you're moving forward structurally.)

II. **Second main point** (this is the second main idea that you mentioned in the preview)
   A. Subpoint
   B. Subpoint

Transition (Verbally tie the second and third main points together to create a sense of forward motion.)

III. **Third main point** (this is the third main idea that you mentioned in the preview)
   A. Subpoint
   B. Subpoint

Conclusion
(This serves the "golden rule" function of telling them "what you told them.")

I. **Thesis Restatement** (You may simply use the Thesis statement from the introduction, changing it to past tense.)

II. **Summarize Main Points** (Remind listeners of the two to three main points about which you elaborated during the speech.)

III. **Clincher** (The clincher serves several functions: provides closure, often ties back to the attention catcher, heightens speech to aid in retention, helps listeners remember...."Thank you" is NOT a clincher.)

References

Refer to the MLA or APA style guide for appropriate citation format.

Standard Speech Outline Template (Label these elements in your TYPED outline)

I. **Attention Catcher**

II. **Establish Relationships**
    A. **Listener Relevance**

    B. **Speaker Credibility**

III. **Preview the Message**
    A. **Thesis Statement**

    B. **Preview**
        1.
        2.
        3.

Body

I. **First main point**

    A. Subpoint

    B. Subpoint

Transition

II. **Second main point**

    A. Subpoint

    B. Subpoint

Transition

III. **Third main point**

    A. Subpoint

    B. Subpoint

Conclusion
I. **Thesis Restatement**

II. **Summarize Main Points**
    1.
    2.
    3.

III. **Clincher**

References
Refer to the MLA or APA style guide for appropriate citation format.

Persuasion Workbook

Outlining Activity

Directions: In the left-handed column below is a partially blank outline from the body of a speech about the history of meteorology. In the right –handed column, arranged in random order are the sub point and sub sub points to fill in the outline. Draw lines to the appropriate sub point or sub sub point for each blank in the outline.

Outline	Sub points and Sub sub points

I. The science of meteorology first developed in ancient Greece.
   A.
   B.
       1.
       2.
	These satellites allow scientists to monitor and predict the weather with greater accuracy than ever before.
	
	The thermometer was invented by Galileo in the 1590's.
	
	Aristotle presented his theories in a book called *Meteorologica*.
	
	In 640 B.C. Thales identified the winter and summer solstices.

II. The Renaissance produced meteorological instruments such as the thermometer and the barometer.
   A.
   B.
	In the 1940's high-speed electronic computers were first used for weather forecasting.
	
	In 1859, for example, Elias Loomis first explained how hurricanes work.
	
	Written around 340 B.C., the *Meteorologica* was the accepted authority on its subject for almost 2,000 years.

III. The 19th century brought major breakthroughs in the understanding and predicting the weather.
   A.
   B.
	The satellites also allow scientists to understand weather dynamics better than ever before.
	
	By 1872, meteorologists could forecast the weather with 75 percent accuracy.
	
	The mercury barometer was created by Torricelli in the 1640's.

IV. The 20th century has made remarkable technological advances in meteorology.
   A.
   B.
       1.
       2.
	Today weather satellites have revolutionized meteorology.
	
	After Thales, Aristotle was the major figure in ancient meteorology.

Patterns of Organization: Ways to organize a speech body

Topical: Several independent points are used to support a thesis
- A. Level of acceptance: move from more accepted to less accepted.
- B. Level of complexity: move from simpler to more complex ideas.
- C. Level of importance: organize according to importance of ideas.
    1. Best foot forward (placing important ideas first)
    2. Best foot last (build up to most important ideas)
    3. Sandwich method (arrange weaker points between stronger points)

Chronological: Arrange ideas according to time logic
- A. Process: first step, second step, third step, etc…
- B. Past/Present/Future
- C. Extended narrative: build speech body around one story

Spatial: Arrange ideas by space logic or physical arrangement

Geographical: Discuss topic according to a map—or different parts of the world

Compare: Focus on similarities between two or more concepts or things

Contrast: Focus on differences between two or more concepts or things
- A. Ideal vs. Real: the way things ought to be versus the way things really are
- B. Myth vs. Fact
- C. Then vs. Now

Division: Divide a topic or object into distinct parts.

Classification: Categorize your subject with objects/concepts of varying types.

Induction: Argument by example

Deduction: Chain of reasoning (from general to specific)

Cause/Effect: Trace out the cause/effect links related to your topic.

Pro/Con: Provide arguments on both sides of a controversial issue.

Problem/Solution: Establish a problem and provide a way to solve the problem.

Monroe's Motivated Sequence: Attention-Need-Satisfaction-Visualization-Action

Question/Answer: Ask a question, then offer a response, etc…

Refutation: Refute audience beliefs until they are left with your belief (often expressed in your thesis).

Process of Elimination: Set up several possibilities and then eliminate all but one.

Statement of Reasons: Identify specific reasons for action and explain each.

Value Criteria: Set up value criteria and show how your topic does or does not meet the established criteria.

Persuasion Outlines:
Policy Propositions

Audience Opinion	Audience Level of Knowledge	Outline Choice The word in CAPS means the speaker is emphasizing this area (possibly with a little more time or supporting material) because the audience needs more emphasis in the area	Emphasis
Neutral	Moderate	Problem Solution (equal time)	Equal
Against	Weak	PROBLEM Solution	Background of Problem
Against	Moderate to strong	Problem SOLUTION	Explain solution more
Against	Strong	Problem CAUSE Solution	Explain CAUSE so audience understands solution
Favorable	Moderate to strong	Monroe's Motivated Sequence	Get audience to take action

How to Prepare a Well-Developed Speech Introduction

An old proverb says, "Well begun is half done." A solid introduction makes your speaking task so much easier because it engages your audience and prepares them for the body of your speech. Without a good introduction, an excellent speech body is practically useless because your audience may tune you out. Here are five tasks of a fully developed speech introduction:

Gain attention: Before launching into your speech, you must first gain the attention of your audience. (You can use an illustration, a startling fact or statistic, a quotation, a joke, a question, or a reference to a recent or historical event.) Make sure your attention getter is interesting, appropriate, and relevant. It should gain favorable attention and lead naturally into your speech topic.

Motivate your audience to listen: After you gain your audience's attention, you must sustain their attention by giving them reasons to listen to your speech. If your thesis is your main point, your motivators are your secondary selling points. What will the audience gain by listening to you? Tell them how your speech will satisfy one or more of their needs. We all have needs related to comfort, safety, control, tradition, relationships, recognition, success, independence, variety, understanding, relaxation, and nurturance. What needs will your speech help fulfill?

Establish your credibility: Let the audience know why you are qualified to speak on your topic. Do you have personal experience or special knowledge related to the topic? Do you have an association with a person or group that gives you insight into the topic? Are you especially committed to the issue you are addressing? Have you carried out research to learn about the topic? Let the audience know why they should give special weight to your words.

State your thesis: A speech needs more than just a general topic: it needs a central assertion to focus and clarify the speaker's main point. Audiences expect to know fairly quickly what a speech is about. Fulfill this expectation by clearly stating your thesis. What precise point do you want to emphasize about your topic?

Preview your speech structure: Oral discourse is more repetitive than written discourse: a speaker needs to repeat his or her main ideas. The speech preview at the end of the introduction "tells the audience what your are going to tell them." The preview allows your listeners to anticipate the main ideas of your speech, which in turn helps ensure that they will remember those ideas after the speech.

How to Prepare a Well-Developed Speech Conclusion

The ancient Greek philosopher Plato said that a speech is like an animal: just as an animal has a head, a body, and a tail, so a speech should have an introduction, a body, and a conclusion. Don't forget to add the "tail" to your speech. Here are four possible tasks of a speech conclusion:

Restate your thesis in a memorable way: If your thesis statement is the main point you are trying to make in your speech, then it is worth saying at least once at the beginning of your speech and once at the end of your speech. Clearly restate your thesis in your speech conclusion in order to "hammer home" your point and cement your thesis in your listener's minds. However, repetition does not have to be boring: restate your thesis *in a memorable way*. (For example, if your thesis was "Smoking causes cancer," your restated thesis could be "Sucking on a cancer stick could put you six feet under.")

Review your main ideas: For a public speech, you need to tell your audience what you will tell them, tell them, and then *tell them what you told them*. Why so much repetition? Because your audience needs a reason to remember what you say: if they hear an idea once, twice, three times, their brains may think it is important enough to stick into long-term memory. Remember, however, that repetition does not have to be boring: use fresh words to review the main ideas of your speech.

Motivate your audience to respond: At the beginning of your speech, you may have motivated your audience to listen to your speech: at the end of your speech, what do you need to motivate them to **do**? If your speech was informative, you could motivate them to remember the new information you have presented. If your speech was persuasive, you may need to motivate them either to take action (a call to action) or to change an attitude, value, or belief (a call to contemplation). As a general rule, the more specific your call to action or call to contemplation is, the more effective your speech will be. Do not speak in vague generalities: tell your audience precisely what they need to do after hearing your speech.

Provide a sense of closure: A speech closer is just as essential as an attention getter. You do not want a long, awkward pause at the end of your speech because your audience does not know that your speech has concluded. Signal the end of your speech with an effective "closer." You may use the same kinds of devices for a closer that work for an attention getter: you can close your speech with an illustration, a startling fact or statistic, a quotation, a joke, a question, or a reference to a recent or historical event. Speakers often use "wrap-around" closers that refer back to the attention getter of their speech: the "wrap-around" closer gives your speech a sense of completion because your speech goes "full circle" and ends where it began.

Supporting materials

Where to use SUPPORTING MATERIALS in your speech
INTRODUCTION

I. Attention Material
    A. SUPPORTING MATERIALS
    B.

II. Establishing Relationships
    A. Listener Relevance
    B. Speaker Credibility

III. Previewing the Message
    A. Thesis
    B. Main Points

BODY

I. Topic Sentence for Main Point I.
    A. SUPPORTING MATERIALS
    B. SUPPORTING MATERIALS
    C. SUPPORTING MATERIALS (if C. is used)

Transition:

II. Topic Sentence for Main Point II.
    A. SUPPORTING MATERIALS
    B. SUPPORTING MATERIALS
    C. SUPPORTING MATERIALS (if C. is used)

Transition:

III. Topic Sentence for Main Point III.
    A. SUPPORTING MATERIALS
    B. SUPPORTING MATERIALS
    C. SUPPORTING MATERIALS (if C. is used)

CONCLUSION

I. Review Thesis
II. Review Main Points
III. Clincher: SUPPORTING MATERIALS

What are SUPPPORTING MATERIALS?

- *Examples and Stories*
  - Factual (verifiable)
  - Hypothetical
- *Surveys*
- *Testimony*
  - Lay
  - Expert
  - Celebrity
- *Numbers and Statistics*
  - Statistics provide a numerical comparison
- *Analogies*
- *Definitions*

Cite your SUPPORTING MATERIALS when they come from a source other than yourself.

What to cite:

- *Author (qualification)*
- *Date*
- *Publication*

Cite it TWICE (or THRICE):

- *ORALLY at point of use*
- *In Works Cited*
- *If using presentation software cite on slides*

Remember to tailor your SUPPORTING MATERIALS to your speaking style

- ***AVOID WRITTEN STYLE***

- ***Rephrase cited information so it flows in ORAL STYLE***

Public Speaking Citations/Resources Standards Sheet

Purpose of oral citations: to show audience members that the information in your speech is legitimate, that you know what you're talking about, and that they should listen to you.

Basic oral citation includes: Title, author, date, relevance of material to the point you are making

When orally citing sources during a speech, use words that make the source valuable to the audience:

Book

Tell more than the title or author's name. Audience members must be convinced that this source is credible (worth paying attention to).

- Do that by <u>building up the author's credentials</u>:
    - Do not say: "In his book ' The Oxford Guide to Library Research,' Thomas Mann says everything cannot be found on the internet."
        - PROBLEM: Who is Thomas Mann? Why should we believe anything he says?
    - Say: "Thomas Mann is the author of "The Oxford Guide to Library Research." Mann is an academic researcher at the doctoral level who served for 20 years as a general reference librarian at the largest library in the world—the Library of Congress. He said that everything cannot be found on the internet."
- OR convince us by <u>building up</u> <u>the book's credentials</u>:
    - "The Oxford Guide to Library Research was published in 2005 and covers more than 290 pages detailing how to find information. The book includes how to use specialized encyclopedias, problems and advantages of keyword searches in the library, and hidden treasures of library material often overlooked by students."

Website

Tell more than the name of the website. Again, audience members must be convinced that this source is credible.

- Do that by <u>building up the organization sponsoring the website</u>:
    - "This website produced by the US government, contains immeasurable amounts of information because the source—the Library of Congress—is the world's largest library. I accessed information on May 23, 2008 from www dot library of congress dot gov. On that site, Library of Congress news releases are posted. One of the Library of Congress press releases, dated May 22, said that…"

References

Mann, T. (2005) *The Oxford guide to library research* (3rd ed.) New York: Oxford University Press.

Urschel, D. & Saladini, R. (2008, May 22). Michael Wesch to discuss "The Anthropology of YouTube" at Library of Congress June 29. *News from the Library of Congress*. Retrieved May 23, 2008 from http://www.loc.gov/today/pr/2008/08-104.html.

Example of Raw Research (Cut and pasted from Ebscohost sources)

On this page you'll see a sample of research pulled directly from articles I found on Ebscohost (before parsing, paraphrasing and citing in oral format) See the next page for an example of the finished research assignment.

True Story:

Health education teacher Pacy Erck remembers what it was like back when Edina High School students had to show up by 7:25 a.m. "The kids were always very tired," she recalls. But these days, Erck rarely has a kid nod off in class. That's because in the fall of 1996, officials at this Minnesota school decided to ring the first bell an hour later, at 8:30 a.m. *Sleep* researchers had reported that teens' natural slumber patterns favor a later bedtime, and the school wanted to ensure that its high schoolers weren't being shortchanged by an early *wake*-up call. The change means that students average five more hours of *sleep* a week, and teachers can see a difference. "You don't have the kids putting their heads down," Erck says. "The class is livelier." (Boyce)

Surprising Fact:

Most of all, losing sleep alters your metabolism, setting the stage for weight gain. Scientists at the University of Chicago have found that a sleep debt of three to four hours over a few days was all it took to provoke metabolic changes that mimicked pre-diabetes. The researchers monitored 11 healthy young adults for 16 consecutive nights in a clinical research center and found that when their sleep was restricted to four hours for six consecutive nights, their ability to keep blood glucose on an even keel declined significantly. (Ward)

Expert Opinion:

Artificial light from computer and television screens tells the brain that it's not time to wind down. "Your body thinks artificial light is daylight-- which prevents the release of melatonin, a *sleep*-inducing chemical," says Susan Zafarlotfi, PhD, director of the Institute for *Sleep*-Wake Disorders at Hackensack University Medical Center. (Pagán)

Statistic:

A trimmer waistline. People who logged 7 to 9 hours a *night* had an average *BMI* of 24.8--almost 2 points lower than the average *BMI* of those who slept less, University of Washington researchers found. Too-little *sleep* may throw off *hormones* that regulate appetite. (Winters)

Works Cited

Boyce, Nell & Brink, Susan. "THE SECRETS OF SLEEP." U.S. News & World Report 17 May 2004: 58-68.
Pagán, Camille Noe. "The Family Sleep Cure." Prevention 2009 January: 155-157.
Ward, Elizabeth M. "Good Night, Sleep Tight. Weight, Immunity And Memory Will Benefit." Environmental Nutrition September 2004: 1-6.
Winters, Catherine. "Sleep! It's Non-negotiable." Prevention February 2009: 18.

Example of Paraphrased Research in Oral Citation Format

True Story:

In their May 17, 2004 US News and World Report article titled, "The Secrets of Sleep", Nell Boyce and Susan Brink tell the story of Pacy Erck, a Health Education teacher at Edina High School in Minnesota. Ms. Erck struggled for years to keep her morning students awake. She says they were "always nodding off". That is, until school officials made a change that helped all of the students at Edina High School get 5 more hours a week of sleep. The change was surprisingly simple: They moved the start of classes from 7:30 to 8:30 in the morning. Erck has seen a dramatic change. She says her students are no longer dropping their heads constantly and classes are "livelier."

Surprising Fact:

Elizabeth Ward reports some startling discoveries in her September, 2004 article for Environmental Nutrition, "Good night, sleep tight. Weight, immunity and memory will benefit,". Ward writes that sleep researchers at the University of Chicago found that missing just 3-4 hours of sleep nightly over less than a week sends people into a metabolic tailspin so severe that they begin to exhibit early signs of diabetes.

Expert Opinion:

In , "The Family Sleep Cure," published in the January 2009 edition of Prevention magazine writer Camille Noe Pagán reveals one cure she learned from Susan Zafarlotfi, PhD, director of the Institute for *Sleep*-Wake Disorders at Hackensack University Medical Center, that will help the whole family sleep. Zafarlotfi cautions that artificial lighting from TV and computer screens confuses our brains, making us think it is still daylight. This prevents the release of a chemical that helps us sleep, melatonin. As a result, we are wakeful, tossing and turning instead of getting the sleep we need.

Statistic:

Catherine Winters warns, in her February 2009 Prevention magazine article, "Sleep. It's non-negotiable", that a lack of sleep can also have a negative effect on our waistlines! She shares a University of Washington study that found that people who get a full night's sleep tend to have a BMI 2 points lower than people who skimp on sleep. The average BMI for both men and women in the US is 28. 2 BMI lower would be 26. For a woman who is 5'5 that would often mean a drop from size 16 to size 12. For a 5'9" man, it would often mean a drop from a 38 waist to a 34 waist.

Works Cited

Boyce, Nell & Brink, Susan. "THE SECRETS OF SLEEP." U.S. News & World Report 17 May 2004: 58-68.
Pagán, Camille Noe. "The Family Sleep Cure." Prevention 2009 January: 155-157.
Ward, Elizabeth M. "Good Night, Sleep Tight. Weight, Immunity And Memory Will Benefit." Environmental Nutrition September 2004: 1-6.
Winters, Catherine. "Sleep! It's Non-negotiable." Prevention February 2009: 18.

Evaluation of Web Information

The more questions you can answer the more reliable the web site.

WHO is the <u>author</u> of the information? WHO is the <u>host or sponsor</u> of the web site?

- What information do they provide about themselves?
- Can you contact them? Is there an e-mail address? Do they list a street address?
- **If you can't tell who is behind it… don't use it!**

WHY was the site created? Does it have a specific <u>purpose</u>?

- Does it state a purpose or mission? What is it? To sell? To inform? To persuade? Other? (Look for an About Us link)
- What type of site is it?
  - .com = commercial
  - .gov = government
  - .edu = educational
  - .net = network
  - .org = non-profit organization
  - ~(tilde) = personal web page

WHAT is the <u>point of view</u>?

- Is there any bias or slant? Or is it neutral?
- Are there links to other viewpoints? Or does it present both sides of the issue?

HOW <u>credible</u> is the source?

- Does the author or organization have expertise on the topic? What education, degrees, or work experience does the author have?
- Who is the intended audience? College students? Consumers? Children?
- Is it scholarly – that is, written by a researcher or expert for a college or academic audience?
- Are the sources credited with a bibliography, works cited list, or references?
- Are there any obvious errors or misinformation? Is it a collaborative site such as Wikipedia to which anyone can post or edit information?

WHEN was it last <u>updated</u>?

- Is the information current? When was it last revised? What is the copyright date?
- Are there many broken links?

WHERE can I find more information?

- What can you find out about the author or site using other Internet sources or library reference materials? Some suggestions are Librarians' Internet Index (www.lii.org). Contemporary Authors. Gale Literature Resource Center, Encyclopedia of Associations and Magazines for Libraries.

Stories or Verbal Illustrations
The ancient Greek philosopher Aristotle classified humankind as "a political (or social) animal." Teachers of public speaking might well call humans "the story-telling animal." A remarkably stable characteristic of humans in every culture and age is their capacity for relating and receiving narratives.

Effective public speakers use stories because they know that a well-told story can gain and sustain attention, generate emotions, and concretely illustrate an abstract assertion or idea.

Hypothetical (fictional) stories: Hypothetical stories are used to describe future events or to place the audience in the middle of a scenario. They should not be used, however, when a factual story would be more effective: why have your audience imagine a drunk-driving accident when there are plenty of heart-wrenching, real-life stories to tell? Also, never try to pass off a hypothetical story as if it were really true—that is called "lying."

Factual stories: Factual stories make an assertion hit home. Your audience may hear the abstract statement "Smoking causes cancer," but this assertion will mean much more to them if you relate how a specific person smoked and then contracted cancer. ("My father, Tom Blackman, smoked two packs of Camels every day for twenty-five years. We learned this past summer that he has less than a year to live due to advanced lung cancer caused by his cigarette addiction.")

Story length: If your entire speech is built around one story, then this story may be developed in some detail. Otherwise, **extended illustrations** are usually no longer than one minute (about six to ten sentences), and **brief illustrations** are fifteen to thirty seconds long (about two to four sentences). Don't let a story get away from you!

Limitations of stories: Stories do not function well as *proof*. A single story, no matter how well told, does not provide sufficient evidence to establish the truth of an assertion. (A skeptical audience would accuse you of making a poor inductive argument or "hasty generalization.") Therefore, when speaking to a skeptical audience, you should use stories sparingly, and you should supplement them with other types of verbal support, such as statistics or expert testimony.

How to tell a good story: To lend a factual story credibility, you should include specific names, dates and places. To bring a story to life, you should paint a "verbal illustration" with vivid descriptors. To generate emotions, you should use appropriate adjectives and adverbs. Build your story up to a climax with effective verbal and nonverbal elements—get your voice and body involved. Most importantly, *make sure that your story has a clear point*. You may state your point either at the beginning or end of your story.

Statistics

Statistics are facts or occurrences represented *by numbers*. Statistics work well for argumentative speeches because you are able to back up abstract generalizations with specific data. Statistics can be used to quantify information, demonstrate trends, and establish cause-effect relationships.

Remember that your statistics are only as good as your sources: you should use unbiased, credible sources for your statistics. (Statistic from the NRA in a pro-gun speech would not be a wise choice if you were speaking to a liberal audience.)

Mark Twain said that there were three kinds of lies, "Lies, damned lies, and statistics." My favorite anonymous quotation for statistics: "Statistics are like bikinis—what they reveal are interesting, but what they conceal are vital." In other words, human beings know that number can be manipulated, so it is a good idea to combine your statistics with other kinds of verbal support, like expert testimony or logical argumentation.

Hints for using statistic effectively:

--Make sure your statistic are representative. Interviewing ten students on a campus is not a large enough sample to make any statistical claims about the general opinions of the entire student population.

--Build up the credibility of your source before presenting your statistic.

--Round off your statistics to make them easier to remember. (Rather than saying, "Of the 493,975 people who smoke, 51.05 percent will contract some form of cancer," say, "Or the approximately one-half million people who smoke, about half will contract some form of cancer.")

--Use statistics sparingly, too many numbers will result in information overload, and your audience will experience the "Charlie Brown" effect: their brains will not be able to keep up, and all they will hear is "Wa wa wa wa."

--When possible, provide visual aids to reinforce your statistics and aid in memory. (You can use bar graphs, pie charts, and other visual representations for numbers.)

--Personalize your statistics and make them mean something to your audience. After presenting a statistic, provide an example to which your audience can relate. ("Last year five million tons of garbage was deposited in United States landfills. If you stacked this garbage three feet high, it would cover the entire states of Washington, Oregon, and California.")

Visual Aids

Why should a speaker use visual aids?
Visual aids can 1) help gain and maintain attention, 2) aid in memory, 3) emphasize points, 4) clarify ideas, 5) reveal a speech structure, 6) add authenticity, 7) enhance a speaker's credibility.

"One of the best known studies of visual aids in speeches assessed the amount of information the audience recalls because of visual aids. The researchers found that when a speech does not include visual aids, the audience recalls 70 percent of the information three hours after the speech. Three days later, they recall only 10 percent of the information. When the same message is delivered with visual aids only, the audience recalls 72 percent after three hours and about 35 percent after three days. **When the message is delivered both in speech and with visual aids, the recall after three hours is 85 percent and after three days 65 percent.** Clearly, visual aids assist with recall."
(Cindy L. Griffin, Invitation to Public Speaking, Thomson/Wadsworth, 2003, p. 323)

Types of Visual Aids:	**Visual Aid Media:**
People	Flip Charts
Objects	Posters
Models	Handouts
Drawings	Chalk and Marker Boards
Photographs	Overhead Transparency
Maps	Video Monitor
Charts/Graphs	Computer Screen
Textual Graphics	

Guidelines for Preparing Visual Aids:

--Select the appropriate visual aids for your presentation
(Consider your audience, the room in which you will speak, your own skill and experience, and your speech objective)
--Make them easy to see
(The audience members in the back of the room should be able to see them without straining.)
--Keep them simple
(Use easy-to-grasp pictures and only a few words on each visual.)
--Prepare them in advance
(Give yourself plenty of time to create attractive, professional visual aids.)

Guidelines for Presenting Visual Aids:

--Rehearse with your visual aids
--Position visual aids for easy access during your presentation
--Display visual aids only while discussing them
--Verbally reinforce your visual aids clearly and concisely
--Talk to your audience, not to your visual aids
--Remember Murphy's Law

Persuasion Workbook

Public Speaking Presentation Aids Standards Sheet

Purpose of presentation aids: to illustrate, explain, clarify or significantly support a main point or other element in your speech outline.

Three kinds of presentation aids:

Audio Aid—can include:

- Music CD
- Natural sound like animal sound, sound of machinery, sound of the ocean, etc.
- A bell you ring or a whistle you blow

Visual Aid—can include:

- Actual object (inanimate or live)
- Model or representation that is either larger or smaller than actual object
- Chart, graph, diagram
- Drawing or photograph

Audio-visual Aid—can include:

- VHS tape
- DVD
- PowerPoint presentation with images and sound

General rules for using presentation aids:

- Make sure the aid adds clarifying, illustrative support to a specific part of your speech. To be effective, the aid should help us understand how something works, make a complicated process simpler, or explain how or why in relation to one of your main points.

- The aid must be presented in the speech along with the point you are trying to illustrate. In a speech about important people in your life, show the picture of your grandmother when you are talking about her. Do not wait until the end of the speech and treat the photo as an add-on to the presentation. Use it where it supports the information you are sharing.

- One of the most important things to remember about presentation aids is that they must be EASILY seen or heard in the back of the room. To test it, tape your visual aid to your garage door. Have someone who hasn't seen the aid before stand at the end of the driveway. Can they read the aid without straining? If not, it's too small.

- During your speech, talk about the aid in detail. Show it long enough for the audience to look at it completely, analyze it and understand it. Presentation aids take time!

- Be sure to practice your speech with your presentation aids. This is how you discover that they don't work, are too hard to hold without help, or don't actually support the information in your speech. Make this discovery at home while you have time to fix it.

- Talk to your audience, not to your presentation aid.

- All aids should be:
    - Easy to see/hear and understand
    - Demonstrative and explanatory
    - Relevant, professional and appropriate
    - Enhancing instead of distracting

Types of Visual Aids

- Photos
    - Minimum size for portrait showing <u>one person</u>: 11" x 14". If multiple people are in the photo, double the size. Putting photos on transparencies is an inexpensive way to increase the size for your audience.
    - Select photos that are clear, easy to see, and illustrate a specific point in your speech.
    - Photos that show action or people are more interesting than photos of inanimate objects like buildings, cars, etc.
    - Talk about the photo in detail, explaining why you selected it and how it illustrates or proves your point.
    - One excellent photo is far better than two or three mediocre ones. Select wisely!
    - Do not use items that are covered in glass or plastic (like a framed photo). The glare on the glass/plastic from the room's lights will make the image nearly impossible to see.

- Charts, graphs, diagrams
    - Keep it simple. Make them easy to understand.
    - Lots of color or images can detract rather than enhance the information in your chart.
    - Carefully explain your chart, graph or diagram. What does each column mean? What is the significance of the information? What point is it trying to make. Explain!
    - The *smallest* font on your charts and graphs should be <u>at least 120 points which is:</u>

This Big

- o Headlines should be even bigger.

Audio-visual aids

- Test the computer, flash drive, DVD, CD or VHS tape on the equipment a few days before you give the presentation. If you discover it doesn't work, you'll have time to change your plans.

- Have a back-up plan or alternative presentation aid. Electricity goes out and machines malfunction at the worst possible moment.

- Before showing video imagery, explain to us what we're going to see and why you selected this video. What point are you trying to make? Tell us before we see it so that we'll be looking for your message as we view the segment.
  - o Be sure to test the volume before class or have a partner in the back of the room signal you that the volume is too loud or not loud enough.

- During audio-visual aid, stand to the side and view it (with interest and enthusiasm) as the audience watches.

Audio aids

- Ask yourself: do they add significantly to the information in my speech?
- Test equipment before speech day!
- Explain what we're going to hear and why . . . and then let us listen.

Presentation aids using Presentation Software
(Microsoft PowerPoint, Open Office Impress, StarOffice Presentation, Prezi, Apple iWork, Keynote, etc...)

When Microsoft created PowerPoint the technology was a breakthrough in presentation software. Before PowerPoint designers had to create large color images on illustration boards, photograph the images and develop the images for slides or transparencies. PowerPoint spread like wildfire because businesses no longer had to hire designers to build their presentations. Unfortunately, when Microsoft created their tutorials for the use of their marvelous new presentation tool they neglected to follow the basic principles of presentation aid construction historically followed by designers (also discussed in the visual aid section on the previous page). In order to use presentation software to create visual aids that will enhance rather than distract from your message follow a few simple rules:

1. Powerpoint isn't a weapon—don't load it with bullets!
   Bullets force you to introduce multiple concepts on a single slide. Introduce only 1 concept per slide in order to reinforce meanings and focus audience interest.
2. Use 1 or 2 striking images on each slide.
3. Use emotion-provoking images.
4. Limit words to labels and headings.
   It is harder for audiences to process information presented simultaneously in oral form and written text--so all those power points that are just text with bullets actually make it harder for audience members to process the information you are presenting! (Pass, 2003)
5. Insert blank black slides when you want your audience to focus on you rather than the screen.
6. Use animation only when the movement will enhance audience understanding.
7. Use sound effects only when the sounds will enhance audience understanding.
8. Embedded video clips should not exceed 30 seconds

A note on presenting with presentation software: Put enough information on your slides so you won't have to use note cards or a manuscript. Look like a pro—use a remote control to advance your slides! Both of the above will allow you to look and sound more comfortable since you won't be juggling multiple items in your hands.

Pass, F. R. (2003). Cognitive Load Theory and Instructional Design: Recent Developments. *Educational Psychologist* , 1-4.

Language

Effective Language Tools for Oral Presentations

Anaphora: Figure of repetition that occurs when the first word or set of words in one sentence, clause, or phrase is/are repeated at the beginning of successive sentences, clauses, or phrases; repetition of the initial word(s) over successive phrases or clauses.

"To raise a happy, healthy, and hopeful child, **it takes** a family; **it takes** teachers; **it takes** clergy; **it takes** business people; **it takes** community leaders; **it takes** those who protect our health and safety. **It takes** all of us." - Hillary Clinton, *1996 Democratic National Convention Address*

Alliteration: Figure of emphasis that occurs through the repetition of initial consonant letters (or sounds) in two or more different words across successive sentences, clauses, or phrases. Two kinds may be distinguished: 1) Immediate juxtaposition occurs when the second consonant sound follows right after the first -- back-to-back. 2) Non-immediate juxtaposition occurs when the consonants occur in nonadjacent words.

"Somewhere at this very moment a child is **b**eing **b**orn in America. Let it be our cause to give that child a **h**appy **h**ome, a **h**ealthy family, and a **h**opeful future." - Bill Clinton, 1992 Democratic National Convention Acceptance Address

Metaphor: Figure of explication occurring when a comparison made by speaking of one thing in terms of another; an implied comparison between two *different* things which share at least one attribute in common; an association between two unlike things (A vs. B) achieved by borrowing the language that refers to thing A and applying it to thing B.

"At the dawn of spring last year, **a single act of terror** brought forth **the long, cold winter in our hearts**. The people of Oklahoma City are mourning still." -- Al Gore, *Oklahoma Bombing Memorial Address*

Simile: Figure of explication in which two things that share at least one attribute are explicitly associated with each other; an overt comparison between two unlike things as though they were similar -- usually with the words "like" or "as".

"Henry was 18 when we met and I was queen of France. **He came down from the north to Paris with a mind like Aristotle's** and **a form like mortal sin**. We shattered the commandments on the spot."-- delivered by Katherine Hepburn (from the movie *The Lion in Winter*)

Antithesis: Figure of balance in which two contrasting ideas are intentionally juxtaposed, usually through parallel structure; a contrasting of opposing ideas in adjacent phrases, clauses, or sentences.

"We observe today not a victory of party but a celebration of freedom, symbolizing **an end as well as a beginning, signifying renewal as well as change**." -- John F. Kennedy, *Inaugural Address*

Parallelism: Figure of balance identified by a similarity in the syntactical structure of a set of words in successive phrases, clauses, sentences; successive words, phrases, clauses with the same or very similar grammatical structure. This figure often occurs public address with others such as antithesis, anaphora, asyndeton, climax, epistrophe, and symploce.

"I've tried to offer leadership to the Democratic Party and the Nation. If, in my high moments, I have done some good, **offered some service**, **shed some light**, **healed some wounds**, **rekindled some hope**, or stirred someone from apathy and indifference, or in any way along the way helped somebody, then this campaign has not been in vain."-- Jesse Jackson, *1984 Democratic National Convention Address*

Enumeratio: Figure of amplification in which a subject is divided into constituent parts or details, and may include a listing of causes, effects, problems, solutions, conditions, and consequences; the listing or detailing of the parts of something.

Kramer: "Who's gonna turn down **a Junior Mint**? **It's chocolate**; **it's peppermint**; **it's delicious**."—Seinfeld

Transitional Words

There is another type of connecting word that you may use between the independent clauses of compound sentence. The words that belong in this group are not co-ordinate conjunctions. They are sometimes called **transitional words** because they are not pure conjunctions.

Some of these words have a slight connecting force. Others have some adverbial force. But they all belong to the independent clause which they introduce or in which they are found. Connectives that belong to this group *are always preceded by a semicolon.*

Since many of these words are regarded as independent elements, they are usually set of by commas. Words like *moreover, however, therefore,* and *nevertheless* are usually set off. Words like *then, still, yet,* and *so* are seldom set off by commas when they retain their adverbial force.

The road was unpaved; **nevertheless**, we drove on in the rain.

I missed the first boat; **however**, I arrived on time.

The President introduced the speaker; **then** he sat down.

Ethel was sick; **in fact** she had one of her usual colds.

We arrived early; **as a result**, we had time to visit with our friends.

We cannot get materials; **consequently**, we cannot finish the job.

I became tired of doing his work; **moreover**, I had my own work to do.

I did not dislike the play; **on the contrary**, I enjoyed it immensely.

When to use Transition Words

Cross out the transition words in each section that you think are overused. Circle at least 2 transition words in each section that you would like to incorporate into your speaking style.

TIME RELATIONSHIPS:
afterwards, meanwhile, at this point, next, eventually, previously, finally, presently, currently, then
CONTINUANCE OF AN IDEA:
additionally, finally, again, further, also, furthermore, and, in addition, as a result, moreover, besides, too, equally important, eventually, at the same time
PROVIDING AN EXAMPLE:
as an illustration, for example, for instance, such as, including, to illustrate
EMPHASIZING A POINT:
again, as a matter of fact, as a result, indeed, in fact, evidently
COMPARISON:
also, like, basically, likewise, in the same fashion, in the same manner, similarly, too, perhaps
CONTRAST:
although, however, and yet, on the contrary, conversely, even though, on the other hand, nevertheless, yet, otherwise
CAUSE AND EFFECT:
as a result, therefore, consequently, thus, for this reason, so, moreover, because
DRAWING A CONCLUSION:
as a consequence, as a result, consequently, for the most part, for these reasons, in conclusion, in other words, in short, on the whole, finally, therefore

Persuasion Workbook

Personal Reporting of Communication Apprehension (PRCA)

DIRECTIONS: This instrument is composed of twenty-four statements concerning feelings about communicating with other people. Please indicate the degree to which each statement applies to you by marking whether you (1) strongly agree, (2) agree, (3) are undecided, (4) disagree, or (5) strongly disagree. Work quickly; record your first impression.

_____ 1. I dislike participating in group discussions.

_____ 2. Generally, I am comfortable while participating in group discussions.

_____ 3. I am tense and nervous while participating in group discussions.

_____ 4. I like to get involved in group discussions.

_____ 5. Engaging in a group discussion with new people makes me tense and nervous.

_____ 6. I am calm and relaxed while participating in group discussions.

_____ 7. Generally, I am nervous when I have to participate in a meeting.

_____ 8. Usually I am calm and relaxed while participating in meetings.

_____ 9. I am very calm and relaxed when I am called upon to express an opinion at a meeting.

_____ 10. I am afraid to express myself at meetings.

_____ 11. Communicating at meetings usually makes me uncomfortable.

_____ 12. I am very relaxed when answering questions at a meeting.

_____ 13. While participating in a conversation with a new acquaintance, I feel very nervous.

_____ 14. I have no fear of speaking up in conversations.

_____ 15. Ordinarily I am very tense and nervous in conversations.

_____ 16. Ordinarily I am very calm and relaxed in conversations.

_____ 17. While conversing with a new acquaintance, I feel very relaxed.

_____ 18. I'm afraid to speak up in conversations.

Persuasion Workbook

_____ 19. I have no fear of giving a speech.

_____ 20. Certain parts of my body feel very tense and rigid while giving a speech.

_____ 21. I feel relaxed while giving a speech.

_____ 22. My thoughts become confused and jumbled when I am giving a speech.

_____ 23. I face the prospect of giving a speech with confidence.

_____ 24. While giving a speech, I get so nervous I forget facts I really know.

Use the scoring formula that follows to calculate your PRCA-24. Then, please report your scores in the table below. Be sure to include your name and date of test.

SCORING: The PRCA permits computation of one total score and four subscores. The subscores are related to communication apprehension in each of four common communication contexts: group discussions, meetings, interpersonal conversations, and public speaking. To compute your scores merely add or subtract your scores for each item as indicated below.

Group Sub Scores

1. Add up your scores from question numbers 2, 4, and 6
2 Add 18 points to the above total.
3. Add up the scores from Questions 1, 3, and 5 and subtract this total from the score in direction 2. This is your apprehension level for Group Discussion. Your score can range from a low of 6 to a high of 30

Meeting Sub Scores:
1. Add scores from 8, 9, and 12.
2. Add 18 points to the above total
3. Add scores from 7, 10, and 11. Subtract this total from the score in direction 2. Your score can range from a low of 6 to a high of 30.

Persuasion Workbook

Interpersonal Conversations
1. Add the scores from questions 14, 16, and 17
2. Add 18 points to the above total.
3. Add the scores from questions 13, 15, and 19 and subtract this total from the total in direction 2. Your score can range from 6 to 30.

Public Speaking
1. Add scores from questions 19, 21, and 23
2. Add 18 points to the above total
3. Add scores from questions 20, 22, and 24. Subtract this total from the total in direction 2. Your score can range from 6 to 30

To determine your overall CA score, add together all four sub scores.
Your score should range between 24 and 120. If your score is below 24 or above 120, you have made a mistake in computing the score.
Scores between **83 and 120** indicate a high level of communication apprehension.
Scores between **55 and 83** indicate a moderate level of communication apprehension.
Scores between **24 and 55** indicate a low level of communication apprehension.

Name
Class and Time
Group sub score
Meeting sunb score
Interpersonal sub score
Public speaking sub score
Total Score (add the four sub scores together)